Properties of Materials

Floating or Sinking

Charlotte Guillain

KT-464-656

ABERDEENSHIRE
LIBRARIES

WITHDRAWN
FROM LIBRARY

ALIS

3014768

www.raintreepublishers.co.uk
Visit our website to find out
more information about
Raintree books.

To order:

☎ Phone 0845 6044371

🖹 Fax +44 (0) 1865 312263

🖳 Email myorders@capstonepub.co.uk

Customers from outside the UK please telephone +44 1865 312262

Raintree is an imprint of Capstone Global Library Limited,
a company incorporated in England and Wales having its
registered office at 7 Pilgrim Street, London, EC4V 6LB
– Registered company number: 6695582

"Raintree" is a registered trademark of Pearson Education
Limited, under licence to Capstone Global Library Limited

Text © Capstone Global Library Limited
First published in hardback in 2009
Paperback edition first published in 2010
The moral rights of the proprietor have been asserted.

All rights reserved. No part of this publication may be
reproduced in any form or by any means (including
photocopying or storing it in any medium by electronic means
and whether or not transiently or incidentally to some other
use of this publication) without the written permission of the
copyright owner, except in accordance with the provisions of
the Copyright, Designs and Patents Act 1988 or under the terms
of a licence issued by the Copyright Licensing Agency, Saffron
House, 6–10 Kirby Street, London EC1N 8TS (www.cla.co.uk).
Applications for the copyright owner's written permission should
be addressed to the publisher.

Edited by Charlotte Guillain and Catherine Veitch
Designed by Joanna Hinton-Malivoire
Picture research by Elizabeth Alexander
Originated by Heinemann Library
Printed by South China Printing Company Limited

ISBN 978 0 431 19350 2 (hardback)
13 12 11 10 09
10 9 8 7 6 5 4 3 2 1

ISBN 978 0 431 19358 8 (paperback)
14 13 12 11 10
10 9 8 7 6 5 4 3 2 1

British Library Cataloguing in Publication Data
Guillain, Charlotte
Floating or sinking. – (Properties of materials)
532'.02
A full catalogue record for this book is available from the
British Library.

Acknowledgements
The author and publishers are grateful to the following for
permission to reproduce copyright material:
Alamy p. **17** (© 81A); © Capstone Publishers pp. **7**, **18**, **19**,
22 (Karon Dubke); Corbis pp. **5** (© Jose Fuste Raga), **6**
(© Andy Newman/epa), **12** (© Frans Lanting); Getty Images pp. **10**
(AFP/Stringer), **15** (Gulfimages), **16** (Richard Elliott/Photographer's
Choice); Photolibrary pp. **4** (Ben Davidson/Animals Animals), **8**, **23**
top (81A Productions), **11**, **23 middle** (Mirko Zanni/WaterFrame
– Underwater Images), **13** (Wolfgang Herath/imagebroker.net), **21**
(J.W. Alker/imagebroker.net); Shutterstock pp. **9** (© mangojuicy), **14**
(© Max Blain), **20**, **23** bottom (© newphotoservice).

Cover photograph of river rafting reproduced with permission of
Shutterstock (© Jörg Jahn). Back cover photograph of a stone sinking
in water reproduced with permission of Photolibrary
(81A Productions).

The publishers would like to thank Nancy Harris and Adriana
Scalise for their assistance in the preparation of this book.

Every effort has been made to contact copyright holders
of any material reproduced in this book. Any omissions
will be rectified in subsequent printings if notice is given to
the publisher.

Contents

Materials that float

Some things float.

Things that float can be flat.

Things that float can be heavy.

Things that float can be light.

Materials that sink

Some things sink.

Things that sink can be light.

Things that sink can be heavy.

Things that sink can be solid.

Materials that float or sink

Wood can float.

Wood can sink.

Metal can float.

Metal can sink.

Paper can float.

Paper can sink.

Glass can float.

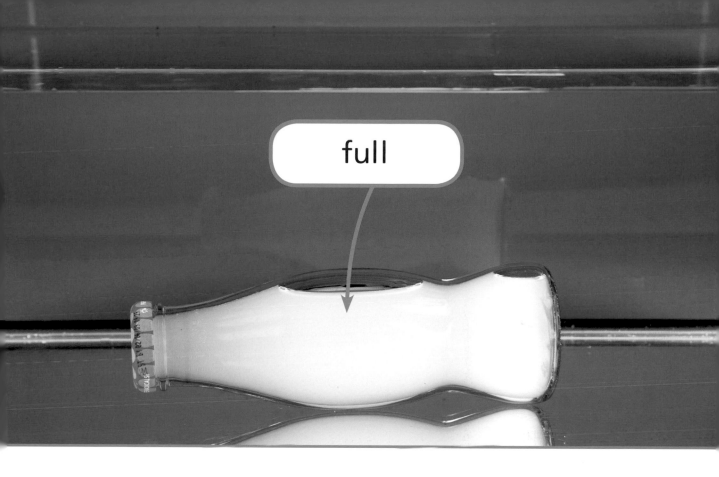

Glass can sink.

surface

Things that float stay on top of the water.

Things that sink go to the bottom of the water.

Quiz

Which of these things float?

Which of these things sink?

Picture glossary

sink drop below the surface of water and go on moving downwards to the bottom

solid fixed shape that is not a gas or a liquid

surface

surface top part of something

Index

Note to parents and teachers
Before reading
Read aloud *Who Sank the Boat?* by Pamela Allen. This book can be used as a springboard to get children motivated about sinking and floating. Tell children materials that float stay on top of water and materials that sink go to the bottom of water. Ask children to describe things they have seen sink or float.

After reading
Give groups of children a bucket of water and a bag with materials – rock, square of paper, straw, foam ball, penny, bath toys, wooden blocks, etc. Place children in groups. Tell them to make predictions and record whether each object will sink or float in water. Children can record their predictions on a pre-made worksheet or in an exercise book. As children place their objects in the water, ask them to observe what happens. When the children have finished exploring sinking and floating objects, ask them the following questions:
1.   "How many of your predictions were correct?"
2.   "Describe the objects that sank. What do they have in common?"
3.   "Describe the objects that floated. What do they have in common?"